WICKED GREEK

BY HOWARD TOMB
Illustrations by Jared Lee

WORKMAN PUBLISHING • NEW YORK

ACKNOWLEDGMENTS

Many thanks to Elizabeth Louise Brown, Vassilios Gargalas and Carbery O'Brien.

Copyright © 1995 by Howard Tomb
Cover photo by Miwako Ikeda/International Stock
All rights reserved. No portion of this book may be reproduced—mechanically, electronically, or by any other means, including photocopying—without written permission of the publisher. Published simultaneously in Canada by Thomas Allen & Son Limited.

Library of Congress Cataloging-in-Publication Data
Tomb. Howard
Wicked Greek for the traveler / by Howard Tomb;
illustrations by Jared Lee.
p.   cm.
ISBN 1-56305-707-7
1. Greek language—Conversation and phrase books—Humor.
2. Greece—Guide books—Humor. I. Title.
PN6231.G87T66   1994
489' .383421—dc20   94-33026
                                                          CIP

Workman books are available at special discounts when purchased in bulk for premiums and sales promotions as well as for fund-raising or educational use. Special editions or book excerpts can also be created to specification. For details, contact the Special Sales director at the address below.

Workman Publishing Company
708 Broadway
New York, NY 10003-9555

Manufactured in the United States of America
10 9 8 7 6 5 4 3 2 1

CONTENTS

WELCOME TO GREECE

GETTING AROUND

CULTURE AND ARTS

WELCOME TO GREECE

For thousands of years, the lure of history has tantalized adventurers and drawn legions of visitors to Greece. Romans, Goths, Slavs, Byzantines, Turks, Germans, Brits, and Yanks all tried to possess the land of the gods, but most ended up badly sunburned or dead.

Today, the birthplace of Western civilization seems foreign to many American and European visitors. Perhaps this is because the Greeks have held on to their culture with a firm grasp, even after we have asked them nicely to speak English and serve us chardonnay.

One shouldn't expect the descendants of Apollo and Athena to pander to the tourist trade, of course, and trying to whip them into shape is futile. Nevertheless, met on their own terms, Greeks are among the warmest people anywhere. What sounds like angry shouting to us may just be a discussion about the weather; genuine arguments usually feature knives.

This book is meant to help Wicked Travelers enjoy the chaos that is Greece while avoiding genuine arguments, being eaten alive by giant one-eyed shepherds or lured to destruction by comely sirens on the beach.

Kali tihi.

PRONUNCIATION GUIDE: IT'S GREEK TO ME!

In *Wicked* phonetics, a ~ means a "y" sound slips in, as in the Spanish *mañana* . The syllable k~ee-oh, for example, is pronounced in one syllable like "kyo." The "g" represents a gagging sound, while the soft "dh" lies lazily between "d" and "th."

Many Greek words are long, and neophytes can get lost in the polysyllabic thickets. Take the name Spirotakalamakamammalapoulis, for example. As in most Greek words, the accent falls on one of the last three syllables: spee-roh-et-CET-eh-rah.

DISCLAIMER

Whereas the Greek gods are not fully dead but only down on their luck, and whereas it is unwise to use the phrases in this book to correct, criticize, insult or woo any god stuck in a dead-end job catering to tourists, the author and his family, agents, publisher, retailers, assorted Furies, and legion of asps take no responsibility whatsoever for any offense to any god or mortal, and hereby refuse to provide one iota of bail money, legal counsel, spells, curses, entreaties, or animal sacrifices on behalf of any reader even if Cerberus himself has a death grip on several of the reader's most cherished body parts.

WELCOME TO THE WORLD'S FIRST THEME PARK

Greece has the oldest amusement parks in the Western world. The ancient Romans found ruins when they first arrived in the Peloponnesos, and many took advantage of groups tours at special rates. Not much has changed since then. Everything is still made of stone, and descendants of the original tour guides still lurk near the ruins of ancient buildings, theaters, statues, agoras, and the odd column, waiting to take a few hundred thousand drachma for a tour.

Is this temple the main attraction?	Ειναι αυτος ο ναος η κυρια ατρακσιον;	*EE-nay ah-FTOHS oh nah-OHS ee kee-REE-ah ah-trah-ks~ee-OHN?*
It's pretty banged up.	Ειναι πολυ στραπατσαρισμενος.	*EE-nay poh-LEE strah-pah-tsah-ree-SMAY-nohs.*
What happened to that caryatid's face?	Τι επαθαν τα πρυσωπα των καρυατιδων;	*Tee AY-pah-than ta proh-ssoh-pa tohn ka-ree-AH-tee-dhon?*
How did that fellow lose his limbs?	Που ξεχασε ο μαγγας τα ξερα του;	*Pue XAY-hah-ssay o MAH-gahs tah xay-RAH tue?*

WELCOME TO GREECE ✸

Hey, look! Up ahead! More marble!	Κοιτα! Και αλλα μαρμαρα!	*KEE-ta! kay AH-lah MAH-rmah-rah!*
I must say it is exciting.	Πρεπει να ομολογησω οτι ειμαι συνεπαρμενος.	*PRAY-pee nah oh-moh-loh-GHEE-soh OH-tee EE-may SEEN-ay-pah-RM AY-nohs.*
But when do we get to see Future World?	Και ποτε θα δουμε τον κοσμο του μελλοντος;	*Kay POH-tay thah DHUE-may tohn KOH-smoh tue MAY-loh-ndohs?*
It's time to head over to the museum.	Εινα ωρα να πηγαινουμε για το μουσειο.	*EE-nay OH-rah nah pee-GHAY-nue-may gh~ee-AH toh mue-SEE-oh.*
I hear they have air conditioning.	Λενε οτι εχει και κλιματισμο!	*LAY-nay oh-tee AY-hee kay klee-mah-tee-SMOH!*

TIMELINE: FIND YOUR ANCESTORS

Year	What Greeks Were Doing	What Other Europeans Were Doing
c. 1500 B.C.	Linear B script developed.	Burfr learns how to spit.
c. 800 B.C.	Homer composes *The Odyssey* and *The Iliad*.	Gloph chases a squirrel.
c. 600 B.C.	Anaximander theorizes humans arose from another species.	Moght notices her boyfriend's bad breath.
447 B.C.	Parthenon completed.	Urml emits a series of grunts.
429 B.C.	Sophocles writes *Oedipus Rex*.	Pidgar makes a hat from mud and twigs.
367 B.C.	Aristotle joins Plato's Academy.	Churlb and his gang sharpen some sticks.
c. 250 B.C.	Eratosthenes calculates the dimensions of Earth to within 1.3 percent.	Horb-kek begins strapping live animals to his body for warmth.

TAXI TO AGONY

The Greeks do not need horror films—they have taxicabs.
The deeper your panic, the faster they'll drive, except in
the impenetrable Athens traffic. Men stop their cars in the
middle of the road to stare at any European or American
woman on foot, and taxi drivers try to romance their fares.
They may also try to pick up additional passengers *en
route* and take you out of your way.

Yes, you're right.	Ναι! Εχεις δικιο.	*Nay! AY-hees DHEE-k~ee-oh.*
I am a goddess.	Ειμαι θεα.	*EE-may thay-AH.*
I do not wish to ride with other passengers.	Δεν θα επιθυμουσα να συνταξιδευσω με αλλους επιβατες.	*Dhayn thah ay-pee-thee-MUE-ssah nah seen-dah-xee-DHAY-fssoh may AH-lues ay-pee-VAH-tays.*

Nor do I wish to visit your cousin's jewelry shop.	Ουτε επιθυμω να επισκεφθω το κοσμηματο-πωλειο του εξαδελφου σου.	*UE-tay ay-pee-thee-MOH nah ay-pee-skay-FTHOH toh koh-smee-mah-toh-poh-LEE-oh tue ay-xah-DAY-lfue sue.*
Slow down or I'll turn you into a sow/lizard/chicken kabob.	Πηγαινε πιο σιγα ειδ'αλλως θα σε μεταμορφωσω σε γουρουνα/ σαυρα/ σουβλισμενο κοτοπουλο.	*PEE-ghay-nay p~ee-OH see-GHAH ee-DHAH-lohs thah say may-tah-moh-RFOH-soh ghue-RUE-nah SAH-vrah sue-vlee-SMAY-noh koh-TOH-pue-loh.*
Make me an offering of your worry beads.	Αφιερωσε μου το κομπολοι σου.	*Ah-fee-ay-roh-SAY mue toh koh-mboh-LOH-ee sue.*
I might tip you/let you live.	Τοτε ισως να σου δωσω φιλοδωρημα/ να σε αφησω να ζησης.	*TOH-tay EE-sohs nah sue DOH-ssoh fee-loh-DOH-ree-mah/nah say ah-FEE-ssoh nah ZEE-sees.*

TURKISH INSULTA-MATIC

Greeks and Turks have been fighting and interbreeding since long before the beginning of recorded history. You can join in the ancient tradition by combining the elementary words below to make your own insults. WARNING: Use these remarks only at a great distance, preferably from another continent.

A	B	C
towel-headed πετσετοκεφαλε *pay-tsay-toh-KAY-fah-lay*	**fig-faced** συκομουρη *see-koh-MUE-ree*	**goat-husband** κατσικοαγα-πητικε *kah-tsee-ko-ah-gha-pee-tee-KAY*
scabby ψωριαρη *psoh-r~ee-AH-ree*	**falafel-eating** φελαφελοφαγε *fay-lah-fay-loh-FAH-ghay*	**prison guard** δεσμοφυλακα *dhay-smoh-FEE-lah-kah*
pathetic μοιρολατρη *mee-roh-LAH-tree*	**black-toothed** μαυροδοντιασ-μενε *mah-vroh-dhoh-nd~ee-ah-SMAY-nay*	**sheep fondler** προβατοαγα-πητικε *proh-vah-toh-ah-ghah-pee-tee-KAY*
swarthy μελαμψε *may-lah-MPSAY*	**camel-humping** καμηλοκα-μπουρη *kah-mee-loh-kah-MBUE-ree*	**rug salesman** εμπορε χαλιων *AY-mboh-ray hah-l~ee-OHN*
landlubbing στεριανε *stay-r~ee-ah-NAY*	**pot-bellied** κοιλαρα *kee-lah-RAH*	**chicken-choker** παλαμοπαιχτη *pah-lah-moh-PAY-htee*

BUST ON THE BUS DRIVER

Due to disparities in guidebook spellings of towns outside Athens, and the inability of drivers to understand English, you will never know where you're going on a bus. To make matters worse, every ride includes hairpin turns through tiny villages at speeds approaching the sound barrier. Sit in front where you can howl directly into the driver's ear.

You're quite a driver.	Εισαι οδηγαρας.	*EE-ssay oh-dhee-GHAH-rahs.*
I thought those widows were history.	Νομιζα οτι δεν υπαρχουν πια χηρες.	*NOH-mee-zah OH-tee dhayn ee-PAH-rhuen p~ee-AH HEE-ray-ss.*
Say, these look like Bronze Age potholes!	Για δες, αυτες οι λακουβες μοιαζουν σαν να ειναι απο την εποχη του χαλκου!	*Gh~ee-AH- dhays ah-FTAYS ee lah-kUE-vays m~ee-AH-zuen sahn nah EE-nay ah-POH teen ay-poh-HEE tue hah-LKUE!*
Is that the Aegean 600 feet below us?	Αυτο, 200 μετρα κατω απο τα ποδια μας ειναι το Αιγαιο;	*Ah-FTOH, dhee-ah-KOH-sah MAY-trah KAH-toh apoh tah POH-dh~ee-ah mahs EE-nay toh ay-GHAY-oh?*

GETTING AROUND 🚗

Is this road wide enough for a bus?	Ειναι αυτος ο δρομος αρκετα-φαρδυς για το λεωφορειο;	*EE-nay ah-FTOHS oh DROH-mohs ah-rkay-TAH- fah-RDHEES gh~ee-AH toh lay-oh-foh-REE-oh?*
Will your plastic saints protect us?	Νομιζεις οτι οι πλαστικοι σου αγιοι θα μας προστατεψουν;	*Noh-MEE-zees OH-tee ee plah-stee-KEE sue AH-ghee-ee thah mahs proh-stah-TAY-psuen?*
Let me off.	Σταματα να κατεβω.	*Stah-MAH-tah nah kah-TAY-voh.*
I'm going to hire myself a mule.	Θα προσλαβω ενα μουλαρι.	*Thah proh-SLAH-voh AY-nha mue-LAH-ree.*

TROJAN ROAD WARRIOR

Poor driving skills and hot tempers make Greek roads notoriously dangerous. Keep in mind that Oedipus killed his father in the first recorded traffic dispute. If you have a rental car and a death wish, fling a few caustic remarks.

Hey, you Turk! Can't you tell right from left?	EEE! Τουρκοσπορε, Σκορδο ρεεε κρεμυδι;	*AYAYAY! Tue-RKOH-spoh-ray, SKOH-rdhoh rayayay! Kray-MEE-dhee?*
You're on the wrong side of the road, marblehead!	Εισαι στην λαθος μερια του δρομου στραβοκεφαλε!	*EE-ssay steen LAH-thohs may-r~ee-AH tue DHROH-mue strah-voh-KAY-fah-lay!*
Your car is uglier than your wife!	Η σακαρακα σου ειναι πιο ασκημη και απο την γυναικα σου!	*Ee sah-kah-RAH-kah sue EE-nay p~ee-OH AH-skee-mee kee ah-POH-teen ghee-NAY-kah sue!*
Do us all a favor and drive home to Ankara!	Κανε μας μια χαρη και τραβα πισω στην Αγκυρα απ'οπου ηρθες!	*KAH-nay mahs m~ee-AH HAH-ree kay TRAH-vah PEE-soh steen AH-ngee-rah ah-POH-pue EE-rthays!*
If you can find the gas pedal!	Εαν βεβαιως μπορεσης να βρης το γκαζι!	*Ay-AHN vay-VAY-ohs boh-REES nha brees toh GAH-zee!*

COMMON ROAD SIGNS

Only desperate people, such as Greeks, even consider driving in Greece. If you must take the wheel, be sure to memorize the meanings of these unique symbols.

OLIVES
NEXT 1500 KM

MYTHICAL
HERO FELL
NEXT LEFT

BATHING
SUITS
REQUIRED

SLOW
WIDOWS

NEXT DEPARTURE FOR
PIRAEUS 2:41 A.M.

CONSULTING THE ORACLE FOR FERRY SCHEDULES

Most Greek travel agents work for particular shipping lines and will not mention the availability—or even the existence—of other lines. The *limenarhion,* the port police, hold the answers you seek. If they aren't available, request an audience with the Oracle at Delphi.

I seek to answer the Riddle of the Ferries.	Προσπαθω να λυσω τον γριφο των πορθμειων.	Proh-spah-THOH nha LEE-soh tohn GHREE-foh tohn poh-RTHMEE-ohn.
In particular, the Mystery of the Next Departure to Patmos.	Για την ακριβεια, το μυστηριο της επομενης αναχωρησεως για την Πατμο.	Gh~eeAH teen ah-KREE-vee-ah, toh mee-STEE-ree-oh tees ay-poh-MAY-nees ah-nah-hoh-REE-ssay-ohs gh~ee-AH teen PAH-tmoh.
Are the ferry gods feeling perky today?	Ειναι οι θεοι των πορθμειων τσαντισμενοι σημερα;	EE-nay ee thay-EE tohn poh-RTHMEE-ohn tsah-ndee-SMAY-nee SEE-may-rah?
We depart at 3 P.M., then?	Τοτε, θα αναχωρησουμε στις 3 μετα μεσημβριαν;	TOH-tee, thah ah-nah-hoh-REE-ssue-may stees trees may-TAH may-ssee-MVREE-ahn?

GETTING AROUND 🚗

Thank you for enlightening me, Insightful One.	Ευχαριστω που με φωτισες Ω! διορατικε.	*Ay-fhah-ree-STOH pue may FOH-tee-ssays OH! dhee-oh-rah-tee-KAY.*
What tribute can I offer?	Τι φορον τιμης μπορω να αποτισω;	*Tee FOH-rohn tee-MEES mbo-ROH nah ah-poh-TEE-soh?*
That seems a little high.	Μου φαινεται τσουχτερος.	*Mue FAY-nay-tay tsue-htay-ROHS.*
Would you accept these magic olive pits?	Θα δεχοσουνα αυτα τα μαγικα κουκουτσια ελιας;	*Thah dhay-HOH-ssue-nah ah-FTAH tah mah-ghee-KAH kue-KUE-ts~ee-ah ay-l~ee-AHS?*

CRUISING IN THE STYX

Charon, who was believed to ferry the spirits of the dead to Hades, represents the archetypal cruise director. Indeed, on many ferries you may feel you are already in hell. If you can, tour a ship *before* paying for a cruise. Otherwise, book your reservations with a travel agent in the U.S. so you'll have someone to sue when you get home. Remember: every island on your itinerary means another night in the Spartan cell of your "cabin."

I paid for a stateroom.	Πληρωσα για δωματιο με θεα.	*PLEE-roh-sah gh~ee-ah doh-MAH-tee-oh may THAY-ah.*
I got a broom closet.	Αυτο που μου δωσατε ειναι πιο μικρο και απο ντουλαπα.	*Ah-FTOH pue mue DOH-ssah-tay EE-nay pee-OH mee-KROH kay ah-POH due-LAH-pah.*
You promised a pool.	Μου υποσχεθηκατε οτι θα ειχε πισινα.	*Mue ee-poh-shay-THEE-kah-tay OH-tee thah EE-hay pee-SEE-nah.*
You gave us a tub of saltwater.	Αφτο που μας δωσατε ειναι μια μπανιερα με θαλασσονερο.	*Ah-FTOH pue mahs DHOH-ssah-tay EE-nay m~ee-AH bah-n~ee-AY-rah may thah-lah-SSOH-nay-roh.*
You said we would arrive at dawn.	Ειπατε οτι θα φταναμε την αυγη.	*EE-pah-tay OH-tee thah FTAH-nah-may teen ah-VGHEE.*

GETTING AROUND

Now I suppose you will ask us to row.	Αυτο που μενει ειναι να μας ζητησετε να τραβηξουμε κουπι.	*Ah-FTOH pue MAY-nee EE-nay nah mahs zee-TEE-say-tay nah trah-VEE-xue-may kue-PEE.*

NAUTICAL DEITIES

Like their ancient forebears, today's sailors rely on natural forces for their progress and safety. Knowing from whom certain blessings flow can give you more confidence at the helm.

God	Province	Suggested Offerings
Atlas	Navigation	Up-to-date nautical charts
Boreas	North wind	Fisherman's sweater
Castor and Pollux	Protector of sailors	Signal flares, life jackets
Helios	The sun	SPF 20, sunglasses
Mercury	Outboard motors	High-quality motor oil
Midas	Mufflers	Valid warranty
Zenith	Radios	Fresh batteries

ISLAND-HOPPING WITH THE GODS

Yachting is simply *the* way to travel among the 50 or so major Greek isles. And renting a boat without a skipper or crew is the only way to experience a genuine odyssey of your own. Before setting sail, familiarize yourself with a few nautical phrases.

Calling all vessels and maritime deities.	Κληση προς ολα τα σκαφη και τις θαλασσιες θεοτητες.	*KLEE-ssee pros OH-la tah SKAH-fee kay tees thah-LAH-ssee-ays thay-OH-tee-tes.*
Mayday, Mayday.	ΣΟΣ, ΣΟΣ.	*Sohs, sohs.*
We are sunburned/lost/seasick.	Ειμαστε καμενοι απο τον ηλιο/ χαμενοι/ εχουμε ναυτια.	*EE-mah-say kah-MAY-nee ap-OH tohn EE-l~ee-oh/ hah-MAY-nee/ AY-hou-me nah-FTEE-ah.*
Poseidon is angry. Repeat. Poseidon is angry.	Ο Ποσειδωνας ειναι θυμωμενος. Επαναλαμβα-νω. Ο Ποσειδωνας ειναι θυμωμενος.	*O poh-ssee-DHOH-nahs ee-nay thee-moh-MAY-nos. Ay-pah-nah-lah-MVAH-noh. O poh-ssee-DHOH-nas EE-nay thee-moh-MAY-nos.*
Our position is _____.	Η θεση μας ειναι.	*Ee THAY-ssee mas EE-nay.*

GETTING AROUND 🚗

Send calamine/ Dramamine/ skilled sailors.	Ω! Ικαρε! Στειλε καλαμινη/ δραμαμινη/ Θαλασσολυκους.	*Oh! EE-kah- ray!STEE-lay kah- lah-MEE-nee/ dhrah-mah-MEE- nee tha-lah-SSOH- lee-kues.*

THE WINDS OF MYKONOS

The island of Mykonos is famous for its windmills, which catch the blasts that blow down from the north. Each wind has a name, depending on its strength. Seafaring people like the *Mykoniots* enjoy talking about the weather; learn a few wind names so you can join the sailors in breezy discussions.

Greek Name	Translation	Sign
kareklatos	*"chair wind"*	chairs blow off *taverna* patios
kambanatos	*"bell wind"*	church bells ring by themselves
magoulatos	*"cheeks wind"*	face begins to flap
skylogyris- menatos	*"dog-rolling wind"*	pets tumble through the streets
tellysavalatos	*"baldness wind"*	hair is ripped out by the roots
pnigmenoko- limbatos	*"learn-to- swim wind"*	small children are launched into the sea

THE WILD TWO

When Pandora opened her box, Greek roads spilled out, along with elderly pedestrians, catatonic barnyard animals staring into space, acres of slippery gravel and nauseatingly high cliffs. If you must rent a motorbike, insist on the proper equipment, pray the Fates will preserve you, and take a partner who can direct traffic around your body.

Is this motorbike equipped with a Virgin Mary?	Εχει το μοτοποδηλατο εικονισμα της Παναγιας;	*AY-hee to moh-toh-poh-DHEE-lah-toh ee-KOH-nee-smah tees pah-nah-gh~EE-ahs?*
How about a helmet, then?	Τι θα'λεγες για κανενα κρανος, τοτε;	*Tee THAH-lay-ghays g~ee-A kah-NAY-nah KRAH-nohs, TOH-tay?*
Will you build me a roadside shrine if I am killed?	Θα μου φτιαξετε κανενα κονοστασι εαν σκοτωθω;	*Tha mue f~ee-AH-xay-tay kah-NAY-nah koh-noh-STAH-ssee ay-AHN skoh-toh-THOH?*
Does that include geraniums?	Θα εχει και γερανια;	*Thah AY-hee kay ghay-RAH-n~ee-ah?*

GETTING AROUND 🚗

OEDIPUS REX'S LONG AND WINDING ROAD

Oedipus had trouble following even the simplest instructions, including a) Never Have Sex with Women Old Enough to be Your Mom, b) Do Not Beat to Death Men Old Enough to be Your Dad, and c) Refrain from Stabbing Yourself in the Eyes. In his later years as a fatherless blind divorcé, Oedipus roamed the Peloponnesos and got lost. Visitors unfamiliar with the Greek alphabet may appreciate the man's troubles.

Can you help us?	Μπορειτε να μας βοηθησετε;	*Boh-REE-tay nah mahs voh-ee-THEE-say-tay?*
We cannot read the signs.	Δεν ξερουμε να διαβαζουμε τα σηματα.	*Dhayn XAY-rue-may nah dh~ee-ah-VAH-zue-may tah SEE-mah-tah.*
We are going mad with confusion.	Μας την εχει δωσει η κατασταση.	*Mahs teen AY-hee DHOH-ssee ee kah-TAH-stah-see.*
Direct us to a travel agent.	Οδηγηστε μας σε ενα πρακτορειο ταξειδιων.	*Oh-dhee-GHEE-stay mahs say AY-na prah-ktoh-REE-oh tah-ksee-DHEE-ohn.*
We want to go home.	Θελουμε να παμε σπιτι μας.	*THAY-lue-may nah PAH-may SPEE-tee mahs.*

PHILOSOPHY 101 B.C.

The foundations of Western philosophy were laid in Greece, as were the philosophers who seduced young men with pretty arguments. Knowing ancient Greek philosophy can still help us approach the ideal graduate student.

SOCRATES (*c.* 470–399 B.C.)

This magnetic Athenian arrived on the philosophy scene just as the Presocratic era came to a close. Rather than lecturing to students, which made them fidget, Socrates walked with them as he asked questions to force them to think in new ways.

His queries included, "Is there an ideal size for pectoral muscles?", "Are you certain you have to go home tonight?", and "If man had invented the telephone, would you give me your home number?"

The "Socratic method" was successful, but its inventor, at age 70, was convicted of corrupting young men. Sentenced to drink hemlock, his last words were, "This is a far, far better drink than retsína."

Socrates left no writing of his own, but his work was recorded by his best student, Plato.

PLATO (*c.* 428–*c.* 348 B.C.)

This Athenian wrote close to thirty "dialogues," many featuring Socrates. Plato struggled to create a logical system of philosophy, but often focused on petty issues and missed the point. According to Plato, for example, if Socrates is a man, and all men have only one toga, then Socrates must go nude on washday. This theory relies on the fallacy that Greek clothing ever gets washed.

In Plato's "middle period," he suggested that all real philosophers must withdraw from everyday life, preferably to his cave, where they could mudwrestle and discover the ideal Form of man.

In his third period, Plato tried to identify ideal ideals and became confused. His best student, Aristotle, stepped in to fill the void.

ARISTOTLE (384–322 B.C.)

Aristotle was born in ancient Macedonia on what is now the Gulf of Rendina. At 17, he wanted to attend one of the big party schools, but his father, the court physician, insisted he attend Plato's Academy. Aristotle graduated *summa cum laude* and spent the next 20 years teaching at the school.

He went on to tutor young Alexander the Great. In 338 B.C., Aristotle returned to Athens and founded his own school, The Lyceum. There he espoused the theory of the golden mean, that everything was fine in moderation, and its corollary, that a fellow should be willing to try anything once. Aristotle seduced enormous numbers of students with this clever theory, but after Alexander fell, anti-Macedonian graffiti drove the philosopher into exile for the rest of his life.

ARISTOPHANES UNPLUGGED

Classical theater resembled today's rock concerts: the audience knew every number by heart, performers wore high heels, loud costumes and heavy makeup, and they relied on backup singers, known as the chorus.  Most of the plays have been lost, but those still extant can be seen in performance in amphitheaters such as the Epìdavrus in the Peloponnesos.

Antigone?	Αντιγνονη;	*Ah-ntee-GHOH-nee?*
We've seen that.	Το εχουμε δει αυτο.	*Toh AY-hue-may dhee ah-FTOH.*
What else is showing?	Τι αλλο παιζει;	*Tee AH-loh PAY-zee?*
Isn't this the Octoplex?	Δεν ειναι εδω το σινε παλας;	*Dhayn EE-nay ay-dhoh toh see-NAY pah-LAHS?*
We were hoping to see *Vampire Lesbians of Sodom*.	Νομιζαμε οτι θα βλεπαμε τις Βρυκολ-ακιασμενες Λεσβιες των Σοδομων.	*Noh-MEE-zah-may OH-tee thah VLAY-pah-may tees vree-koh-lak~ee-ah-SMAY-nays lay-SVEE-ays tohn soh-DHOH-mohn.*

CULTURE AND ARTS 🏛

ZEUS, MIGHTY PLAYGOD

Yes, some Greek men do look like gods, but before you're overwhelmed by their appearance, consider their former god-in-chief, Zeus.

When a deity becomes all-powerful, they would have you believe, monogamy is out of the question and incest is officially approved. After Zeus married Hera, his fantastically nasty sister, he tried to have sex with almost every creature in the universe, from top goddesses to stray chickens.

He took the forms of animals himself to woo people with exotic tastes.

And sometimes, to throw Hera off the scent of his infidelity, Zeus turned his lovers into cows after he finished with them. He tried to kill thousands of his children.

Once you know what it means to love a "Greek god," you may want to reconsider the charms of the typical mortal. He  may not be able to take the form of a white bull for an evening, but neither will he turn you into a heifer.

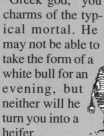

FLIRTING WITH DANGER

Many Greek men, like their Mediterranean brothers, are jealous and possess hot tempers. When addressing their wives, sisters and daughters, be prepared to run for your life.

Will you be my vestal virgin?	Θες να γινης η εστιαδα παρθενα μου;	*Thays nah GEE-nees ee ay-stee-AH-dhah pah-RTHAY-nah mue?*
You would tend my eternal flame.	Θα επιστατεις την ασβεστη φλογα μου.	*Thah ay-pee-stah-TEES teen AH-svay-stee FLOH-gah mue.*
I would pay for your orthodontia/ electrolysis.	Θα πληρωσω για την ορθοδοντικη/ ηλεκτρολυση σου.	*Thah plee-ROH-ssoh gh~ee-AH teen oh-rthoh-dhoh-ndee-KEE/ ee-lay-KTROH-lee-see sue.*
Ah! Here is your father! He does not look happy.	Α! Να και ο πατερας σου! Δεν φαινεται Και χαρουμενος.	*Ah! nah kay oh pah-TAY-rahs sue! Dhayn FAY-nay-tay kay hah- RUE-may-nohs.*
I will go quickly now to fetch your toga.	Θα παω τωρα αμεσως να φερω τον τηβεννο σου.	*Tha PAH-oh TOH-rah ah-MAY-ssohs nah FAY-roh ton TEE-vay-NOH sue.*

CULTURE AND ARTS 🏛

MEDEA: WHAT A BITCH!

Just as Zeus is a model for Greek men, Medea remains the feminine ideal. She refused to play the role of victim. She didn't trust her stepson, for example, and tried to poison him at her dinner table. She used magic to help Jason steal her father's Golden Fleece and then ran away with the handsome Argonaut. To slow her dad's pursuit, she sprinkled the route with her brother's body parts. Ten years later, when Jason left her for another woman, she sent her rival a toxic gown and slit her own children's throats. If you wrong a Greek woman, you'll need some smooth talk.

You are mistaken, darling.	Κανεις λαθος αγαπη μου.	*KAH-nees LAH-thohs ah-GHA-pee mue.*
I *admire* your mustache.	Θαυμαζω το μουστακι σου.	*Thah-VMAH-zoh toh mue-STAH-kee sue.*
You look nothing like a horse to me.	Δεν μου μοιαζεις καθολου για αλογο.	*Dhen mue m~ee-AH-zees kah-THOH-lue gh~ee-AH AH-loh-ghoh.*
I would never betray you.	Δεν θα σε προδωσω ποτε μου.	*Dhen tha say proh-DHOH-soh poh-TAY mue.*
I want to go on living.	Η ζωη ειναι γλυκεια.	*Ee zoh-EE EE-nay ghlee-k~ee-AH.*

SAINT OLYMPICS

The Olympics were held in Greece for a thousand years, but they have now been replaced by saints' feast "days." Festivities begin on the eve of the saint's day and extend through the  next day and into the night. It takes superb coordination and godlike stamina to keep partying. Encouraging words can come in handy.

It is early yet!	Ειναι νωρις ακομα!	*EE-nay noh-REES ah-KOH-mah!*
The sun won't come up for another hour!	Ο ηλιος θελει καμια ωρα ακομα για να ανατειλη!	*Oh EE-l~ee-ohs THAY-lee kah-m~ee-AH OH-rah ah-KOH-mah gh~ee-AH nah ah-nah-TEE-lee!*
We'll dance until noon!	Θα χορεψουμε μεχρι το μεσημερι!	*Thah hoh-RAY-psue-may MAY-hree toh may-ssee-MAY-ree!*
Bring us another case of wine!	Φερε μας ακομα μια κασα κρασι!	*FAY-ray mahs ah-KOH-mah m~ee-AH KAH-sah krah-s~EE!*

CULTURE AND ARTS 🏛

Hey, Hercules! How about some stuffed grape leaves!	Εε! Ηρακλη! Τι θα ελεγες για μερικους ακομα ντολμαδες!	*Ayay! ee-rah-KLEE! Tee thah AY-lay-ghays g~ee-AH may-ree-KUES ah-KOH-mah doh-LMAH-dhays!*
What's the matter, my friend?	Τι επαθες φιλε μου;	*Tee AY-pah-thays FEE-lay mue?*
You can't sit down now!	Δεν μπορεις να κατσης τωρα!	*Dhayn boh-REES nah KAH-tsees TOH-rah!*
Let's smash beer bottles!	Να σπασουμε μπουκαλια μπυρας!	*Nah SPAH-ssue-may bue-KAH-l~ee-ah BEE-rahs!*
Push-ups in the broken glass. Yes!	Καμψεις αναμεσα στα σπασμενα γυαλια Ναι!	*KAH-mpsees ah-NAH-may-ssah stah spah-SMAY-nah gh~ee-ah-l~ee-AH nay!*
Give the man an olive crown!	Δωσε του ανθρωπου εναν κοτινο ελαιας!	*DHOH-ssay tue ah-NTHROH-pue AY-nahn KOH-tee-noh ay-LAY-ahs!*

DIVINING THE HOTEL RATING SYSTEM

Greek hotels are officially rated A, B, C, D, or E based not on qualitative issues but on amenities like running water and the variety of insects. Government-run establishments, known as *xenònes,* are dull but reliable. More adventurous travelers sometimes choose *domàtia,* which are essentially spare bedrooms in people's homes. No matter where you want to stay, however, it's always wise to ask a few questions before handing over your traveler's checks.

Will I have to share my room with people/ scorpions/snake-haired witches?	Θα πρεπει να μοιραστω το δωματιο μου με αλλους ανθρωπους/σκο ρπιυυς/ μαγισες που εχουν φιδια στα μαλλια;	*Thah PRAY-pee nah mee-rah-STOH to dhoh-MAH-tee-OH mue me AH-lues ah-NTHROH-pues/skoh-rp~ee-U ES/MAH-ghee-ssays pue AY-huen FEE-dh~ee-ah stah mal~ee-AH?*
Does it come with a plastic statue of Achilles, or must I supply my own?	Θα εχει και κανενα πλαστικο αγαλμα του Αχιλλεα, η θα πρεπει να φερω το δικο μου;	*Thah AY-hee kay kah-NAY-nah plah-stee-KOH AH-ghah-lmah tue ahee-LAY-ah, ee thah PRAY-pee nah FAY-roh to dhee-KOH mue?*

THE PRACTICAL TRAVELER 🧳

Will I be sharing any walls with Pan/newlyweds?	Μηπως θα μενη ο Παναας/τιποτα νεονυμφοι στο διπλανο δωματιο;	*MEEH-pohs thah MAY-neeh oh PAH-nahs/TEEH-poh-tah neh-OH-neeh-mfee stoh dhee-plah-NOH dhoh-MAH-tee-oh?*
Is there an exciting all-night *taverna* on the premises?	Υπαρχει καμια ενδιαφερουσα διανυκτερευου-σα ταβερνα στα περιξ;	*Eeh-PAH-rhee kah-MEE-ah eh-ndhee-ah-FAY-rue-ssah dhee-ah-nee-ktay-RAY-vue-ssah tah-VAY-rnah stah PAY-reex?*
Do you let lazy pagans lie in bed all morning?	Αφινετε τους οκνηρους ειδωλολατρες να μενουν στο κρεββατι ολο το πρωι;	*Ah-FEE-nayh-tay tues oh-knee-RUES eeh-dhoh-loh-LAH-trays nah MAYH-nuen stoh kreh-VAH-tee OH-loh toh proh-EE?*
Is there somewhere else to stay in this town?	Υπαρχει κανενα αλλο μερος σ'αυτην την πολη για να μεινη κανεις;	*Ee-PAH-rhee kah-NAY-nah AH-loh MAY-rohs sah-FTEEN teen POH-lee g~eeh-AH nah MEE-nee kah-NEES?*

LABYRINTH OF THE CHEAP TRINKETS

Greece has been producing tacky souvenirs for several thousand years. Even the Byzantines went home with embarrassing *flokáti* rugs and *tagária* shoulder bags. Each area has its specialties: Santorini is known for inexpensive gold reproductions, for example, and Athens boasts the original flea market. Caveat emptor: you'll have to carry—or throw overboard—whatever you buy.

I do like this style of imitation tile/plate/ amphora.	Μου αρεςει αυτο το ειδος της απομιμησεως στα κεραμικα/ πιατα/στους αμφορεις.	*Mue ah-RAY-see ah-FTOH toh ee-dhohs tees ah-poh-mee-MEE-ssay-ohs stah kay-rah-mee-KAH/ pe-AH-tah/stues ah-mfoh-REES.*
But the nude youth depicted is unimpressive.	Αλλα ο γυμνος νεος που απεικονιζεται, δεν μου γεμιζει το ματι.	*Ah-LAH oh ghee-MNOHS NAY-ohs pue ah-pee-koh-NEE-zay-tay, dhen mue gay-MEE-zee toh MAH-tee.*
Do you have one with a larger javelin?	Εχετε κανενα με μεγαλυτερο ακοντιο;	*AY-hay-tay kah-NAY-nah may may-ghah-LEE-tay-roh ah-KHOH-ndee-oh?*

THE PRACTICAL TRAVELER 📷

This Bacchus corkscrew is a classic.	Αυτο το ελκυφελειο με τον Βακχο ειναι απο τα κλασσικα.	*Ah-FTOH toh ay-lkee-FAY-lee-oh may tohn VAH-khoh EE-nay ah-POH tah klah-ssee-KAH.*
It fits in my luggage.	Χωραει στηνβαλιτσα μου.	*Hoh-RAH-ee steen vah-LEE-tsah mue.*
And I can use it to fend off horny men.	Και μπορω να το χρησιμοποιησω για να απομακρυνω διεγερμενους αντρες.	*Kay mboh-ROH nah toh hree-ssee-moh-pee-EE-soh gh~ee-AH nah ah-poh-mah-KREE-noh dee-ay-ghay-RMAY-nues AH-ndrays.*

REACH OUT AND TOUCH SOMEONE AT RANDOM

The tiny yellow kiosks called *periptera* have four useful items: cigarettes, aspirin, antacid and eccentric pay phones that will often connect you with total strangers. Go with the flow.

Who is this?	Μα ποιος ειναι;	Mah p~ee-OHS EE-nay?
I must have the wrong number.	Πρεπει να εχω λαθος αριθμη,	PRAY-pee nah AY-hoh LAH-thohs ah-ree-THMOH.
What's the best *taverna* near the Plaka?	Ποια ειναι η καλυτερη ταβερνα στην Πλακα;	Pee-AH EE-nay ee kah-LEE-tay-ree tah-VAY-rnah steen PLAH-kah?
Yes, I'll meet you there at 10.	Ενταξει, θα συναντηθουμε εκει στις δεκα.	Ay-NTAH-xee thah see-nah-ndee-THUE-may ay-KEE stees DAY-kah.
I will be easy to spot.	Δεν θα δυσκολευτης να με αναγνωρισης.	Dhayn thah dee-skoll ay-FTEES nah may ah-nah-ghnoh-REE-sees.
I'll be wearing a sunburn.	Θα φοραω κοκκινα εγκαυματα.	Tha foh-RAH-oh KOH-kee-nah ay-CAH-vmah-tah.

BLUE WATER, RAW GARBAGE

The sparkling waters of the Aegean may look fine on a post-card, but Greeks have been throwing things into the sea since they began walking upright. Scuba diving is strictly forbidden because you might steal some of the really old debris. Swimming can be risky because of the fresh stuff. Ask for recommendations.

Do people swim here?	Κολυμπαει ο κοσμος εδω;	*Koh-lee-MBAH-ee oh KOH-smohs ay-DHOH?*
How many survive?	Ποσοι επιζουν;	*POH-see ay-pee-ZUEN?*
Where do the locals swim?	Που κολυμπανε οι ντοπιοι;	*Pue koh-lee-MBAH-nay ee DOH-p~ee-ee?*
Are they alarmed by the sight of shaved legs?	Χτυπαει συναγερμος με την θεα ξυρισμενων ποδιων;	*Htee-PAH-ee see-nah-ghay-RMOHS may teen THAY-ah xee-ree-SMAY-nohn poh-d~ee-OHN?*

VISITING ANCIENT RELICS AND THEIR WIVES

People look old before their time in Greece because they work extremely hard and have no dental coverage. Endless nights of dancing and drinking also take their toll, building up laugh lines and causing hearing loss. When speaking to elders, keep the conversation light.

How's it hanging, Gramps?	Πως παει παππου;	*Pohs pah-ee pah-PUE?*
I said, YOU LOOK WELL!	Ειπα οτι ΦΑΙΝΕΣΑΙ ΜΙΑ ΧΑΡΑ!	*Ee-pah oh-tee FAY-nay-say m~ee-AH hah-RAH!*
Your smell is overpowering!	Η ευωδια σου ειναι αφοπλιστικη!	*Ee ay-voh-dhee-AH sue EE-nay ah-foh-plee-stee-KEE!*
I said, HOW IS YOUR MULE?	Ειπα, ΤΙ ΚΑΝΕΙ ΤΟ ΜΟΥΛΑΡΙ ΣΟΥ;	*EE-pah, tee KAH-nee toh mue-LAH-ree sue?*
YOU TREAT THAT ANIMAL WELL!	ΒΝΕΠΟ ΤΟ ΠΕΡΙΠΟΙΗ-ΣΑΙ ΤΟ ΖΩΝΤΑΝΟ!	*VLAY-poh toh pay-ree-pee-EE-say toh zoh-ndah-NOH!*

THE PEOPLE

I HEAR GRANDMA IS JEALOUS!	ΛΕΝΕ ΟΤΙ Η ΓΙΑΓΙΑ ΖΗΛΕΥΕΙ!	*LAY-nay OH-tee h g~ee-ah-g~ee-AH zee-LAY-vee*
I said, YOUR WIFE MISSES YOU!	Ειπα οτι ΛΕΙΠΕΙΣ ΤΗΣ ΓΥΝΑΙΚΑΣ ΣΟΥ!	*EE-pah OH-tee LEE-pees tees ghee-NAY-kahs sue!*

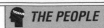

SICK O' STUCCO

When chatting with islanders, you may want to make a pleasant comment or two about the ubiquitous whitewash.

I love what you've done with this house.	Το εχεις κανει κουκλα το σπιτι σου.	Toh AY-hees KAH-nee KUE-klah toh SPEE-tee sue.
How did everyone happen to pick the same charming color?	Πως εγινε και ολοι στο νησι βαψατε τα σπιτια σας με το ιδιο χαριτωμενο χρωμα;	Pohs AY-ghee-nay kay OH-lee stoh nee-SEE VAH-psah-tay tah SPEE-t~ee-ah sahs may toh EE-dhee-oh hah-ree-toh-MAY-noh HROH-mah?
You've even painted the rocks and tree trunks!	Μα εσεις εχετε βαψει μεχρι τις πετρες και τα δεντρα!	Mah ay-SEES AY-hay-tay VAH-psee MAY-hree tees PAY-trays kay tah DAY-ndrah!
They're certainly sanitary now!	Οπωσδηποτε ολα αυτα βοηθαν στην υγιεια!	Oh-pohs-DHEE-poh-tay OH-lah ah-FTAH voh-ee-THAH-nay steen ee-GHEE-ah!
Once you paint the flowers in your garden, you'll be done!	Υποθετω οτι για να τελειωσης πρεπει να βαψεις και τα λουλουδια του κηπου σου!	Ee-poh-THAY-toh OH-tee gh~ee-AH nah tay-lee-OH-sees PRAY-pee nah VAH-psees kay tah lue-LUE-dh~ee-ah tue KEE-pue sue

THE PEOPLE

WHAT ALL THE WIDOWS WILL BE WEARING THIS SUMMER

Rural Greeks wear black on black. Elders prefer the classic look of the 19th century, while teens wear styles from the 1960s and '70s, including some fluorescent green and orange. Most people own only one of each item: one pair of pants, one shirt, and one sweater. They will be flattered if you comment on their choices.

Where *did* you find that outfit?	Που το βρηκες αυτο το φορεμα;	*Pue toh VREE-kays ah-FTOH toh FOH-ray-ma?*
It looks just like wool/cotton/ leather!	Μοιαζει να ειναι απο μαλι/βαμβακι/ δερμα!	*M~ee-AH-zee nah EE-nay ah-POH mah-LEE/vah-MVAH-kee/ DHAY-rmah!*
Thanks, but I'd rather not trade.	Ευχαριστω, αλλα θα προτιμουσα να μην συνδιαλλαγω.	*Ay-fha-ree-STOH, ah-LAH thah proh-tee-MUE-ssah nah meen see-ndhee-ah-lah-GHOH.*
My husband is still alive.	Ο συζυγος μου ειναι ακομα ζωντανος.	*Oh SEE-zee-GHOS mue EE-nay ah-KOH-ma zoh-ndah-NOHS.*

I'm allergic to polyester/ mothballs.	Ειμαι αλλεργικος στον πολυεσθερα/την ναφθαλινη.	*EE-may ah-lay-rghee-KOHS stohn poh-lee-ay-STHAY-rah/teen nah-fthah-LEE-nee.*
Day-glo colors make me look/feel ill.	τα ελεκτρικ χρωματα με κανουν να φαινομαι/αι-σθανομαι αρρωστος.	*Tah ay-lay-KTREEK HROH-mah-tah may KAH-nuen nah FAY-noh-mai/ ay-STHAH-noh-may AH-roh-stohs.*

HANGIN' WITH THE HOMIES

You'll always find a handful of old Greek men whiling away their days in a local *kafenío*. The establishment probably won't serve edible food, but you can get tiny cups of the hot tar they call coffee—and stares from the regular customers. Western women aren't specifically unwelcome, but then neither are Martians.

I'll have a decaf mocha-mint double latté.	Θα παρω ηια ημι-αποκαφενοποι-ημενη μοκα-μεντα με διπλο γαλα.	*Tha PAH-roh mee-ah ee-mee-ah-poh-kah-fay-noh-pee-ee-MAY-nee MOH-kah MAY-ndah may dhee-PLOH.*
Okay. Espresso.	Ενταξει. Εσπρεσο.	*Ay-NDAH-xee. Ay-SPRAY-ssoh.*
No thank you.	Οχι ευχαριστω.	*OH-hee ay-fhah-ree-STOH.*
I passed up that sandwich three days ago.	Και πριν τρεις μερες θα μπορουσα να ειχα φαει εκεινο το σαντουιτς.	*Kay preen trees MAY-rays thah boh-RUE-ssah nah EE-hah FAH-ee ay-KEE-noh toh SAH-ndue-eets.*

Hey, which of you came up with that Trojan horse idea?	Λοιπον, σε ποιον απο σας κατεβηκε η ιδεα του Δουρειου ιππου;	Lee-POHN, say pee-OHN ah-poh SAHS kah-TAY-vee-kay ee ee-DHAY-ah tue DHUE-ree-ue EE-pue?
Hmm. It's awfully quiet in here.	Πολυ ησυχια εχει εδω περα.	Poh-LEE ee-see-HEE-ah AY-hee ay-DHOH PAY-rah.
So. Can I buy you fellows a drink?	Παιδια, θα μου επιτρεπατε να σας κερασω ενα ποτο;	Pay-dh~ee-AH, tha mue ay-pee-TRAY-pah-tay nah sahs kay-RAH-soh AY-nah poh-TOH?
I knew I could make friends in Greece!	Τοξερα οτι θα μπορουσα να κανω φιλους στην Ελλαδα!	TOH-xay-rah OH-tee tha boh-RUE-sah nah KAH-noh FEE-lues steen ay-LAH-dhah!

THE PEOPLE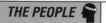

THE GREEK WAY OF LOVE: DIVISION OF MANLY AFFECTION

Just because Greek men sit on each other's laps doesn't mean they won't go home to their wives eventually. If a native gets too friendly with you, say no gracefully.

I am genuinely flattered.	Ειμαι πραγματικα κολακευμενος.	*EE-may prah-gmah-tee-KAH koh-lah-kay-VMAY-nohs.*
You have a god-like physique/odor/gold tooth.	Εχεις θεικο παραστημα/μυρωδια/χρυσο δοντι.	*AY-hees thay-ee-KOH pah-RAH-stee-mah/mee-roh-dh~ee-AH/hree-SSOH DHOH-ndee.*
Unfortunately, I can't stay.	Δυστυχως, δεν μπορω να μεινω.	*Dhee-stee-HOHS dhayn boh-ROH nah MEE-noh.*
My boat/bicycle/chariot will be leaving in five minutes.	Η βαρκα μου/το ποδηλατο μου Το αρμα μου φευγει σε πεντε λεπτα.	*Ee VAH-rkah mue/toh poh-DHEE-lah-TOH mue toh AH-rmah mue FAY-vghee say PAY-nday lay-PTAH.*
I have a pressing engagement/devoted spouse/severe rash.	Εχω μια επειγουσα υποθεση/αφοσιωμενο συζυγο/επικινδυνο εξανθημα.	*AY-hoh m~ee-AH ay-PEE-ghue-ssah ee-POH-thay-ssee/ah-foh-see-oh-MAY-noh SEE-zee-ghoh/ay-pee-KEE-ndhee-noh ay-XAH-nthee-mah.*

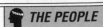

THE GREEK WAY OF LOVE: DIVISION OF CLASSICAL COUPLING

Travelers looking for romance may need a few modern phrases. Many Greeks today are intensely homophobic, however, so be wary. An oblique pickup style may give you plausible deniability.

Excuse me. Could you direct me to the Temple of Dionysus?	Συγγνωμη, θα μπορουσατε να μου πειτε πως να παω στον ναο του Διονυσου;	*See-GHNOH-mee, thah boh-RUE-ssah-tay nah mue PEE-tay pohs nah PAH-oh STOHN nah-OH tue dh~ee-oh-NEE-ssue?*
Would you care to join me in a tribute?	Θα θελατε να με συνοδευσετε σε μια αποτιση φορου τιμης;	*Thah THAY-lah-tay nah may see-noh-DHAY-fsay-tay say MEE-ah ah-POH-tee-ssee FOH-rue tee-MEES?*
Are you at all familiar with architecture?	Εχετε καθολου γνωσεις αρχιτεκτονι-κης;	*AY-hay-tay kah-THOH-lue GHNOH-ssees ah-rhee-tay-ktoh-nee-KEES?*
I'd like you to take a look at something.	Θα ηθελα να κοιταγατε κατι.	*Thah EE-thay-lah nah kee-TAH-ghah-TAY KAH-tee.*

THE PEOPLE

Would you say this is Doric, Ionic or Corinthian?	Τι νομιζετε ειναι αυτο, Δωρικο, Ιωνικο η Κορινθιακο;	*Tee noh-MEE-zay-tay, EE-nay ah-FTOH, dhoh-ree-KOH, ee-oh-nee-KOH, ee koh-ree-nthee-ah-KOH?*
You are at a Golden Age.	Βρισκοσαστε στην Χρυση εποχη.	*Vree-SKOH-sah-stay steen hree-SSEE ay-poh-HEE.*
I would like to do some classical reenactments.	Θα ηθελα να κανω μερικες κλασσικες αναπαραστα-σεις.	*Thah EE-thay-lah nah KAH-noh may-ree-KAYS klah-ssee-KAYS ah-nah-pah-rah-STAH-ssees.*
You be the grateful slave.	Μικρε, εσυ θα παιξης τον ευγνωμονα σκλαβο.	*Mee-KRAY, ay-SSEE thah PAY-xees tohn ay-VGHNOH-moh-nah SKLAH-voh.*
I'll be the benevolent God.	Εγω θα παιξω τον καλοκαγαθο Δια.	*Ay-GHOH thah PAY-xoh tohn kah-loh-KAH-ghah-thoh DHEE-ah.*

PAGAN PRAYER

O Aphrodite, I humbly entreat your assistance in catching the eye of that tanned, athletic-looking Finn anointed with oil on the big white blanket down the beach. I devoutly wish the Finn should lose all good sense for long enough to find me attractive and return to my cheap hotel room for an all-night tribute to your glory, O incomparable bare-breasted goddess. And we would be particularly grateful if you could procure for us a quart of Finlandia, your highness, if you wouldn't mind. And a bucket of ice would be awfully nice, too. Thank you very, very much.

Oohh! Afroditi, tapina se iketevo na kanis na me prosexi afti i athlitiki filandeza, pou einai alimeni me ladi, kai ine xaplomeni epano se ekini tin aspri kouverta kato stin paralia. Me evlavia efhome i filandeza na hasi ta logika tis ke na me vri arketa elkistiko ke na epistrepsoume mazi sto domatio tou xenodohiou mou, gia enan olonih-tio foro timis stin doxa sou, ohh! asigriti gim-nostithi thea. Kai tha sou imoun evgnomon ean mas promitheves me ena boukali finlandia, ipsisti, ean den sou ekane kopo, ke enan kou-va me pago. Episis, ena zevgari hiropedes tha mas epefte poli orea. Se efharisto para para poli.

FOOD, WINE & ENTERTAINMENT

POINT 'N' TZATZÍKI

Greek menus are notoriously inaccurate. To make matters worse, many of them are in Greek. Experienced diners simply ignore them altogether. Instead, they go into the kitchen and point at the things they want, which are swimming in enormous pans filled with olive oil and tomato paste.

What is this?	Τι ειναι αυτο;	*Tee EE-nay ah-FTOH?*
An eggplant–related item?	Ενα μελιτζανοη–αντικειμενο;	*AY-nah may-lee-tzah-noh–a-ndee-KEE-may-noh?*
Lamb and lamb by-products?	Αρνι, και υποπροιοντα αρνιου;	*Ah-RNEE, kay ee-poh-proh-ee-OH-ndah ah-rn~ee-UE?*
What mythical creature lurks beneath the surface?	Ποιο μυθικο πλασμα παραμονευει κατω απο την επιφανεια;	*P~ee-OH mee-thee-KOH PLAH-smah pah-rah-moh-NAY-vee KAH-toh ah-POH teen ay-pee-FAH-nee-ah?*
How recently was it captured/killed?	Ποσο προσφατα το πιασαν/το σκοτωσαν;	*POH-ssoh PROH-sfah-tah TOH p~ee-AH-sahn/toh SKOH-toh-ssahn?*

≋ FOOD, WINE & ENTERTAINMENT

I'll take one of these and two of those.	Θα παρω ενα απο αυτα και δυο απο εκεινα.	*Thah PAH-roh AY-nah ah-POH ah-FTAH kay DHEE-oh ah-POH ay-KEE-nah.*
Please remove the head/eyes/squid parts.	Παρακαλω, βγαλτε το κεφαλι/τα ματια/τα κρεμασταρια.	*Pah-rah-kah-LOH, VGHAH-ltay toh kay-FAH-lee/tah MAH-t~ee-ah/tah kray-mah-STAH-r~ee-ah.*
Make sure I get absolutely none of that substance right there.	Βεβαιωσου οτι δεν θα καταναλωσω καθολου απο αυτην την ουσια εδω.	*Vay-vay-OH-ssue OH-tee dhayn thah kah-tah-nah-LOH-ssoh kah-THOH-lue ah-POH ah-FTEEN teen ue-SSEE-ah ay-DHOH.*

WHACKING THE SQUID

On a touristy island like Ios, the freshness of the *psária* (fish) may vary, but away from the beaten path, it is almost always superb. Seafood may be ordered fried, baked or boiled. Feel free to visit a restaurant's aquarium and mark a creature for death. Agree on a price before cooking. For the freshest possible seafood, choose a live squid from the tank and have the staff beat it to death on the floor while you watch.

YOUR WAITER AND CHAOS

Greek waiters won't clear away the cold congealed food on your table since that's how they served it to you in the first place. Plus, during the hours you wait for new courses to appear from the kitchen, you may get hungry enough to pick at the leftovers. In the meantime, pointed comments may speed the service.

Hey Hermes!	Εε! Ερμη!	*Ay-h! ay-RMEE!*
Get those winged feet in motion!	Κουνα τα φτερωτα σου ποδια!	*KUE-nah tah ftay-roh-TAH sue POH-dh~ee-ah!*
Ah! Sustenance at last.	Επι! τελους θρεπτικες ουσιες.	*Ay-pee! TAY-lues thray-ptee-KAYS ue-SSEE-ays.*
Wait. We didn't order this.	Περιμενε. Δεν παραγειλαμε αυτο.	*Pay-REE-may-nay. Dhayn pah-rah-GEE-lah-may ah-FTOH.*
We want the appetizer *before* the main course.	Θελουμε τα ορεκτικα πριν το κυριως γευμα.	*THAY-lue-may tah oh-ray-ktee-KAH preen toh kee-REE-ohs GHAY-vmah.*
This fish is cold.	Το ψαρι ειναι κρυο.	*Toh PSAH-ree EE-nay KREE-oh.*

🍵 FOOD, WINE & ENTERTAINMENT

Throw it back in the wine dark sea.	Ριξε το πισω στην σκοτεινη θαλασσα.	*REE-xay toh PEE-ssoh steen skoh-tee-NEE THAH-lah-ssah.*
Bring us something hotter than room temperature.	Φερε μας κατι που να ειναι πιο ζεστο απο τον αερα.	*FAY-ray mahs KAH-tee pue nah EE-nay p~ee-OH zay-STOH ah-POH tohn ah-ay-rah.*
And one more thing, my friend.	Και ακομα κατι.	*Kay ah-KOH-mah KAH-tee.*
We'd like to eat before the rosy-fingered dawn.	Θα θελαμε να φαμε πριν φεξει η ροδαλη αυγη.	*Thah THAY-lah-may nah FAH-may preen FAY-xee ee roh-dhah-LEE ah-VGHEE.*

THE UGLY TRUTH ABOUT RETSINA

Ouzo, clear liqueur that turns cloudy when water or ice is added, is drunk throughout the day. Retsína, a resinated wine, is imbibed with meals, and no matter how hard you try, there is no escaping it. As a well-traveled aesthete, of course, you may want to make a few pithy comments about it while you drink.

Excuse me, waiter.	Γκαρσον, με συγχωρεις.	*Gah-RSOHN, may see-ghhoh-REES.*
This tastes like a handful of pine needles.	Αυτο εχει γευση πευκοβελονας.	*Ah-FTOH AY-hee GAY-fsee pay-fkoh-vay-LOH-nahs.*
Do you have a decent scotch?	Εχετε κανενα σκοτς της προκοπης;	*AY-hay-tay kah-NAY-nah skohts tees proh-koh-PEES?*
I see.	Καταλαβα.	*Kah-TAH-lah-vah.*
Perhaps a pint of Mad Dog?	Ισως κανενα μισοκιλο Μαντ ντογκ;	*EE-ssohs kah-NAY-nah mee-SSOH-kee-loh mahd dohg?*
Okay. Bring us your finest bottle of mouthwash.	Ενταξει. Φερε μας το πιο καλο μπουκαλι μαουθουος.	*Ay-NDAH-xee. FAY-ray mahs toh p~ee-OH kah-LOH bue-KAH-lee mah-ueth-ue-ahs.*

OLIVE DRAB

Legend has it that Athena gave olive trees to the Greeks as a reward. It was one of the last they got. Few things grow in the dry, rocky soil of Greece, so shopping for food is easy.

That onion you have for sale looks superb.	Αυτο το κρεμμυδι που πουλας με εκπτωση φαινεται να ειναι νοστιμοτατο.	*Ah-FTOH toh kre-MEE-dhee pue pue-LAHS may AY-ktpoh-see FAY-nay-tay nah EE-nay noh-stee-MOH-tah-toh.*
I'll take it.	Θα το αγορασω.	*THAH toh ah-ghoh-RAH-ssoh.*
And you have *two* kinds of olives? Wow.	Πω Πωω! Εχετε δυο ειδων ελιες;	*Poh poh! AY-hay-tay DEE-oh ee-DOHN ay-l~ee-AYS?*
You know, I want tonight's dinner to be special.	Ξερετε, θελω το σημερινο δειπνο να ειναι κατι το διαφορετικο.	*XAY-ray-tay THAY-loh toh see-may-ree-NOH DEE-pnoh nah EE-nay KAH-tee toh dee-ah-fo-ray-tee-KOH.*
Give us a can of tomato paste.	Δωσε μας μια κονσερβα τοματοπελτε.	*DHOH-say mahs mee-AH koh-NSAY-rvah toh-mah-toh-pay-LTAY.*

REAL MEN DON'T FOLK DANCE

The average New World man hesitates to dance the *hasápiko* with swarthy guys who don't speak English. Nevertheless, they may insist. Unlucky visitors are forced to dance the *zeibèkiko*—solo—or the *tsiftetèli*, the belly dance made famous by Anthony Quinn in "Zorba the Greek." A few excuses may help you delay your performance until you are sufficiently drunk.

No, thank you.	Οχι, ευχαριστω.	*OH-hee ay-fhah-ree-STOH.*
I don't do the goat dance.	Δεν χορευω τον χορο της κατσικας.	*Dhayn hoh-RAY-voh tohn hoh-ROH tees kah-TSEE-kahs.*
I don't even like goats.	Ουτε καν μου αρεσουν οι κατσικες.	*Ue-tay kahn mue ah-RAY-ssuen ee kah-TSEE-kays.*
Besides, I have no mustache.	Εξ αλλου, δεν εχω καν μουστακι.	*Ay-XAH-lue, dhayn AY-hoh kahn mue-STAH-kee.*
I make it my policy not to hold hands with other men.	Εχω σαν αρχη μου να μην κραταω χερια με αλλους ανδρες.	*AY-hoh sahn ah-RXEE mue nah meen krah-TAH-oh HAY-r~ee-ah may AH-llues AH-ndrays.*
But I'll help you break the dishes.	Ομως θα σε βοηθησω να σπασεις τα πιατα.	*OH-mohs thah say voh-ee-THEE-sso nah SPAH-sees tah p~ee-AH-tah.*

🍲 *FOOD, WINE & ENTERTAINMENT*

CREATING A BOUZOÚKI-FREE ZONE

The difference between *tavernas* and *bouzouxìdika* is blurred in Greece; you can just as easily get *calamari* in a music hall as deafened in a *taverna*. *Tavernas* are family places, and *bouzouxìdika* are mostly for guys who like to dance together. Regardless of the distinction, most visitors spend at least one evening in Bouzoúki World. Escaping from that planet may require stern measures.

What an unforgettable sound!	Τι αλησμονητος ηχος!	*Tee ah-lee-SMOH-nee-tohs EE-hohs!*
It's like giant insects mating in August /hell/Asia Minor!	Ειναι οπως οταν γιγαντια εντομα συνουσια- ζονται τον Αυγουστο/στην κολαση/στην Μικρα Ασια!	*EE-nay OH-pohs OH-tahn gee-GHAH-ndee-ah AY-ndoh-mah see-nue-ssee-AH-zoh-nday tohn AH-vghue-stoh/steen KOH-lah-ssee/steen mee-KRAH ah-SSEE-ah!*

FOOD, WINE & ENTERTAINMENT

Or perhaps they are only quarreling.	Η ισως απλως να τσακωνονται.	*Ee EE-ssohs ah-PLOHS nah tsah-KOH-noh-nday.*
May I try it?	Μπορω να δοκιμασω;	*Boh-ROH nah dhoh-kee-MAHS-soh?*
Gadzooks! I have smashed it to pieces!	Αμαν! Το εκανα κομματια!	*Ah-MAHN! Toh AY-kah-nah koh-MAH-t~ee-ah!*
What a pity!	Συμφορα!	*See-mfoh-RAH!*
No more bouzoúki tonight!	Τερμα το μπουζουκι για σημερα!	*TAY-rmah toh bue-ZUE-kee gh~ee-AH SEE-may-rah!*

PARTY-CRASHING TIPS

Greeks are friendly and generous to strangers; after all, you might be a god in disguise. Inserting yourself into their evening *kèfi* is ridiculously easy. All you have to do is ask. Dinner begins at 9 or 10, and the celebration heats up around *dòdeka* (midnight).

May we join you?	Μπορω να κατσω μαζι σας;	*Boh-ROH nah KAH-tsoh mah-ZEE sahs?*
You're too kind.	Ειστε πολυ ευγενεις.	*EE-stay poh-LEE ay-vghay-NEES.*
No, I couldn't eat your food.	Οχι, δεν θα μπορουσα να φαω το φαγητο σας.	*OH-hee, dhayn thah boh-RUE-sah nah FAH-oh toh fah-ghee-TOH sahs.*
It is delicious.	Ειναι εξαιρετικο.	*EE-nay ay-xay-ray-tee-KOH.*
I couldn't drink another glass.	Δεν θα μπορουσα να πιω κι αλλο ενα ποτηρι.	*Dhayn thah boh-RUE-ssah nah p~ee-OH k~ee-AH-loh AY-nah poh-TEE-ree.*
If you insist.	Εαν επιμενετε.	*Ay-AHN ay-pee-MAY-nay-tay.*

FOOD, WINE & ENTERTAINMENT

I wonder if they serve grilled lobster in this restaurant.	Αναρωτιεμαι εαν σερβιρουν ψητο αστακο σ'αυτο το εστιατοριο.	*Ah-nah-roh-t~ee-AY-may ay-AHN say-RVEE-ruen psee-TOH ahstah-KOH sah-FTOH toh ay-stee-ah-TOH-ree-oh.*
Dance? Of course.	Να χορεψω; Μα βεβαιως.	*Nah hoh-RAY-psoh? Mah vay-VAY-ohs.*
Just give me one more minute with this moussaká.	Ενα λεπτο μονο να τελειωσω τον μουσακα.	*AY-nah lay-PTOH MOH-noh nah tayl~ee-OH-ssoh tohn mussah-KAH.*

🍲 FOOD, WINE & ENTERTAINMENT

THE LIQUID SALUTE

After the day's hard physical work is done, every moment is cause for celebration. To join the festivities, where a toast is made each time glasses are filled, learn the following lines.

To your health!	Στην υγεια σου!	*Steen ee-gh~ee-AH sue!*
To Helen, that brunette bombshell!	Στην υγιεια της Ελενης, της εκρηκτικης μελαχρινης!	*Steen Ee-gh~ee-AH tees ay-LAY-nees tees ay-kree-ktee-KEES may-lah-hree-NEES!*
May she forever launch the ships of our hearts!	Ειθε, παντα να κυβερναη τα καραβια της καρδιας μας!	*EE-thay, PAH-ndah nah kee-vay-RNAH-ee tah kah-RAH-v~ee-ah tees kardh~ee-AHS mahs!*
To ancient Troy, may we reclaim it from Turkish dogs!	Στην υγιεια της αρχαιας Τροιας, ειθε να την παρουμε πισω απο τα σκυλια τα Αγαρηνα!	*Steen ee-gh~EE-ah tees ah-RHAY-ahs TREE-ahs, EE-thay nah teen PAH-rue-may PEE-soh ah-POH tah skee-l~ee-AH tah ah-ghah-ree-NAH!*
To Greece!	Στην υγιεια της Ελλαδας!	*Steen Eegh~ee-AH tees ay-LAH-dhahs!*
Where the men are beautiful!	Εκει που οι αντρες ειναι ομορφοι!	*Ay-KEE pue ee AH-ndrays EE-nay OH-moh-rfee!*

FOOD, WINE & ENTERTAINMENT

And the women work like mules!	Και οι γυναικες δουλευουν σαν σκυλια!	*Kay ee ghee-NAY-kays dhue-LAY-vuen sahn skee-l~ee-AH!*

NECTAR OF THE DEMI-GODS

With about 9,000 years of experience in fermenting liquids, Greeks have come up with several that contain alcohol. The recent discovery of refrigeration has been a boon to thirsty travelers, as these beverages can now be chilled to the point where their flavors are blunted. WARNING: If you overdo it, Greeks will give you their cure for hangovers. This substance, known as *patsá,* contains the internal organs of dead sheep.

Beverage	Color	Flavor	Special Features
Demestica	red or white	wine-like	none
Mavrodadfini	red	grape	popular with children
Zitsa	red	cola	bubbles
oúzo & water	white	licorice	comes with appetizers
retsína	yellow	turpentine	contains no turpentine
raki	clear	kerosene	may be fatal

THE INEVITABLE THANK-YOU NOTE

The true adventurer befriends natives while traveling, and the wise one writes them *grámma efharistìria* (thank-you notes). This kind of diligence is rewarded with treats like far-flung pen pals and free food and lodging on future visits. As an added bonus you will be able to eat huge meals at a steep discount in the many New York restaurants owned by your Greek friends' relatives.

NOTE: Letters and cards are more effective when the author makes a sincere attempt to use the native language. The following are phrases commonly needed in this type of correspondence.

Thank you for inviting me for dinner.	Ευχαριστω για την προσκληση σε δειπνο.
It was an epiphany.	Ηταν αποκαλυψη.
This squid was flowing.	Τα καλαμαρια κολυμβουσαν.
The wine was fresh.	Το κρασι ηταν φρεσκοτατο.
Thanks for leaving the thread back to my hotel.	Ευχαριστω που αφησες την πετονια στο ξενοδυχειο μου.

FOOD, WINE & ENTERTAINMENT

Sorry I slew the man with the bull's head.	Συγγνωμη που εσφαξα τον ανδρα με το κεφαλι του ταυρου.
I didn't know he was your cousin.	Δεν γνωριζα οτι ηταν ο εξαδελφος σου.
I shall return one day.	Θα ξαναρθω παλι μια μερα.
I'll try not to fly too close to the sun.	Θα προσπαθησω να μην πεταω κοντα στον ηλιο.
Sincerely yours,	Ειλικρινα δικος σας,